All About Us

ALSO BY PHILIPP KEEL

Splash, Steidl

State of Mind, Nieves

Keel's Simple Diary – Volume Two, TASCHEN

Keel's Simple Diary – Volume One, TASCHEN

AISA – Images of an Imaginary Continent, Edition Judin

Color, Steidl

All About Me – The Teenage Edition, Crown Archetype

All About My Cat, Crown Archetype

All About My Dog, Crown Archetype

Look at Me, Edition Stemmle/Abbeville Press

All About Me – Millennium Edition, Crown Archetype

All About Me, Crown Archetype

PHILIPP KEEL

All About Us

HARMONY BOOKS

NEW YORK

At the outset, I would like you to know that I am not an expert when it comes to relationships. I think we all share a curiosity about the ways in which people interact, and over the years I have found myself wondering about the relationships in my orbit—my parents', my friends', my own. What is it that draws two people together? What is it that keeps people together? What breaks them apart? The answers are infinite and most often complex. And as we all know, there is a secret language between two people that is rarely expressed—to the outside world and often even between the partners themselves. I do not wish to unbalance this mystery. The questions in this book should draw us into a deeper understanding of who we are and how we love.

However you approach this book—with your partner, or individually, imagining how your partner would respond—you should do so with a spirit of adventure and fun. It is not the intention of the book to provoke arguments and controversy. Allow yourself to skip questions. Be wise, generous, and fearless. At times, it may seem as if you are going in two different directions, but in fact you are heading down the same road. Together you will make incredible discoveries and once more become aware that love remains the greatest mystery. As it should.

—Philipp Keel

CONTENTS

Today's date: _____

Do you and your partner plan to go through this book together?   ( ) Yes ( ) No

If yes, who will be "A" and who will be "B"?

A, your name: _____

B, your name: _____

Your dates of birth:

A: _____   B: _____

Your astrological signs:

A: _____   B: _____

If you are "B," did you think for a second that you would
have preferred to be "A"?   ( ) Yes ( ) No

If you are going through this book by yourself, do you plan to
answer for both you and your partner?   ( ) Yes ( ) No

If yes, will you show your partner your answers?   ( ) Yes ( ) No

Which of the following choices best describes your reason for going through this book?

A: ( ) You communicate in silence   ( ) It's your anniversary
      ( ) You are drunk   ( ) You are curious   ( ) You are suspicious
      ( ) Whatever happened to sex?   ( ) Don't ask

B: ( ) You communicate in silence   ( ) It's your anniversary
      ( ) You are drunk   ( ) You are curious   ( ) You are suspicious
      ( ) Whatever happened to sex?   ( ) Don't ask

As a child, what were your first words?

A: _____   B: _____

What did you want to be when you grew up?

A: _____

B: _____

What was your first job?

A: _____   B: _____

What did you do with the money you earned?

A: _____   B: _____

When did you leave home?

A: _____   B: _____

Who or what has had the greatest influence in your life?

A: _____   B: _____

Your professions:

A: _____   B: _____

Would you mind looking at each other for one minute?

    A: ( ) Yes ( ) No   B: ( ) Yes ( ) No

If yes, put this book away.

When did you meet?

A: _____   B: _____

Where did you meet?

A: _____

B: _____

How did you meet?

A: _____

B: _____

What did you think when you saw your partner for the first time?

A: _____

B: _____

Who made the first move?   ( ) A ( ) B

What words did you introduce yourself with?

A: _____

B: _____

How soon after meeting your partner did you begin to have erotic thoughts?

A: _____   B: _____

Who dared the first kiss?   ( ) A ( ) B

Before spending your first night together, what was your concern?

A: _____

B: _____

Did you imagine how it would feel to wake up next to each other?

    A: ( ) Yes ( ) No   B: ( ) Yes ( ) No

How much time elapsed between your first and second date?

A: _____

B: _____

Did the one who promised to call, call when promised?

    A: ( ) Yes ( ) No   B: ( ) Yes ( ) No

Was the first night everything you dreamed of?

    A: ( ) Yes ( ) No   B: ( ) Yes ( ) No

If no, what was missing?

A: _____

B: _____

If yes, what made it so special?

A: _____

B: _____

Have you known true love?

    A: ( ) Yes ( ) No   B: ( ) Yes ( ) No

Are you prepared to accept whatever this book may reveal?

    A: ( ) Yes ( ) No   B: ( ) Yes ( ) No

What is your current state of mind?

A: _____

B: _____

What is happiness?

A: _____

B: _____

What would you like to outlaw in your relationship?

A: _____

B: _____

In exchange for the above, what are you willing to permit in your relationship?

A: _____

B: _____

What problem of your partner's did you think you could solve when you first met?

A: _____

B: _____

Three words that best describe your partner:

A: 1 _____   2 _____   3 _____

B: 1 _____   2 _____   3 _____

Three words that best describe yourself:

A: 1 _____   2 _____   3 _____

B: 1 _____   2 _____   3 _____

What is the best thing about being a woman?

A: _____

B: _____

What is the best thing about being a man?

A: _____

B: _____

What is the quality you find most appealing in a woman?

A: _____   B: _____

What is the quality you find most appealing in a man?

A: _____   B: _____

In a relationship, there are phases when you are more in love and less in love.

    A: ( ) Yes ( ) No   B: ( ) Yes ( ) No

In which phase do you find yourself now?

    A: ( ) More in love   ( ) Less in love   ( ) Neither
    B: ( ) More in love   ( ) Less in love   ( ) Neither

When was the last time you and your partner truly addressed your problems?

    A: ( ) A week ago   ( ) A few months ago   ( ) A year or more ago
    B: ( ) A week ago   ( ) A few months ago   ( ) A year or more ago

What do you find most appealing physically about your partner?

A: _____   B: _____

What do you find most appealing emotionally about your partner?

A: _____   B: _____

What would you like to change about your partner at this very moment?

A: _____

B: _____

If you could start your relationship over again,

    A: ( ) you would.   ( ) you wouldn't.

    B: ( ) you would.   ( ) you wouldn't.

Describe an ideal day with your partner:

A: _____

B: _____

Two of your habits that drive your partner crazy:

A: 1 _____

      2 _____

B: 1 _____

      2 _____

What is the first image that spontaneously comes to mind when you think about your partner?

A: _____

B: _____

How much time do you spend in the bathroom on an average day?

A: _____   B: _____

Choose the two things you miss most in your relationship:

A: ( ) More time for yourself   ( ) Traveling   ( ) More time with your partner
( ) Good conversation   ( ) Your partner's smile   ( ) Dreaming together
( ) Your partner's curiosity   ( ) Your partner's support   ( ) Little surprises
( ) A long vacation   ( ) Dinners and parties   ( ) A month without kids
( ) Passion   ( ) Laughing together   ( ) Spontaneity   ( ) Excitement
( ) Romantic moments   ( ) A sense of discovery

B: ( ) More time for yourself   ( ) Traveling   ( ) More time with your partner
( ) Good conversation   ( ) Your partner's smile   ( ) Dreaming together
( ) Your partner's curiosity   ( ) Your partner's support   ( ) Little surprises
( ) A long vacation   ( ) Dinners and parties   ( ) A month without kids
( ) Passion   ( ) Laughing together   ( ) Spontaneity   ( ) Excitement
( ) Romantic moments   ( ) A sense of discovery

A fantasy that has recently been on your mind:

A: _____

_____

_____

B: _____

_____

_____

FAVORITES

Although you may not wish to make a decision, just give it a try.

Who is your hero?

A: _____   B: _____

Your favorite nickname

    A: for yourself: _____   for your partner: _____

    B: for yourself: _____   for your partner: _____

If you are married, what was your favorite moment of your wedding?

A: _____

B: _____

The sexiest person in the world (other than your partner):

A: _____   B: _____

The nationality most alien to you:

A: _____   B: _____

An erotic book, film, or piece of music:

A: _____

B: _____

The most romantic moment of your current relationship:

A: _____

B: _____

The facial expression of your partner's that you like best:

A: _____

B: _____

The member of your partner's family you like best:

A: _____   B: _____

The friend of your partner's you like best:

A: _____   B: _____

FAVORITES

When you looked your best:

A: _____

B: _____

The place you feel most at home:

A: _____   B: _____

Your favorite waste of time:

A: _____

B: _____

Your favorite way to tease your partner:

A: _____

B: _____

How you cool down after a fight most quickly:

A: _____

B: _____

Your favorite holiday:

A:　( ) Halloween　( ) Pentecost　( ) Ramadan　( ) Martin Luther King Day
　　( ) Chinese New Year　( ) Christmas　( ) Hanukkah　( ) Thanksgiving
　　( ) Passover　( ) Memorial Day　( ) Purim　( ) Kwanza　( ) Easter
　　( ) Rosh Hashanah　( ) Fourth of July

B:　( ) Halloween　( ) Pentecost　( ) Ramadan　( ) Martin Luther King Day
　　( ) Chinese New Year　( ) Christmas　( ) Hanukkah　( ) Thanksgiving
　　( ) Passover　( ) Memorial Day　( ) Purim　( ) Kwanza　( ) Easter
　　( ) Rosh Hashanah　( ) Fourth of July

How would you like to die?

A: _____　B: _____

Your favorite thing to find in the refrigerator:

A: _____　B: _____

Your favorite destination for a vacation:

A: _____　B: _____

Your favorite part of making love:

A: _____

B: _____

The worst time you have had on a date:

A: _____

B: _____

Blind dates are the safest way to meet new people.

      A: ( ) Yes   ( ) No   B: ( ) Yes   ( ) No

A friend you will never allow to arrange a blind date for you:

A: _____   B: _____

A disastrous blind date:

A: _____

B: _____

A blind date that was a pleasant surprise:

A: _____

B: _____

Which movie title best describes your most dramatic breakup?

A:	B:
( ) *Last Tango in Paris*	( ) *Last Tango in Paris*
( ) *Dirty Dishes*	( ) *Dirty Dishes*
( ) *Keep My Grave Open*	( ) *Keep My Grave Open*
( ) *Take the Money and Run*	( ) *Take the Money and Run*
( ) *Young and Innocent*	( ) *Young and Innocent*
( ) *Dr. No*	( ) *Dr. No*
( ) *The Long Goodbye*	( ) *The Long Goodbye*
( ) *Whose Life Is It Anyway?*	( ) *Whose Life Is It Anyway?*
( ) *Rain Man*	( ) *Rain Man*
( ) *My Life to Live*	( ) *My Life to Live*
( ) *Throne of Blood*	( ) *Throne of Blood*
( ) *King of Masks*	( ) *King of Masks*
( ) *Duck Soup*	( ) *Duck Soup*
( ) *Rio Grande*	( ) *Rio Grande*
( ) *Boomerang*	( ) *Boomerang*
( ) *Born Free*	( ) *Born Free*
( ) *And the Ship Sails On*	( ) *And the Ship Sails On*
( ) *The Gold Rush*	( ) *The Gold Rush*
( ) *Kindergarten Cop*	( ) *Kindergarten Cop*
( ) *Apocalypse Now*	( ) *Apocalypse Now*
( ) *The Gods Must Be Crazy*	( ) *The Gods Must Be Crazy*

What was the first thing you noticed about your partner when you met?

A: _____

B: _____

A mistake you made in a previous relationship that you dare not repeat in your current relationship:

A: _____

B: _____

Was there a time when you would have liked to have had a baby but circumstances did not allow it?

    A: ( ) Yes   ( ) No   B: ( ) Yes   ( ) No

Do you regret that you didn't date more before your present relationship?

    A: ( ) Often   ( ) Sometimes   ( ) Never

    B: ( ) Often   ( ) Sometimes   ( ) Never

How old were the oldest and youngest people you have had sex with?

    A: Oldest: _____   Youngest: _____

    B: Oldest: _____   Youngest: _____

You knowingly dated a bitch or a jerk.

    A: ( ) Yes ( ) No   B: ( ) Yes ( ) No

If yes,

A: for how long? _____   B: for how long? _____

A: for what reason? _____   B: for what reason? _____

You have drawn blood in a fight with an ex.

    A: ( ) Yes ( ) No   B: ( ) Yes ( ) No

Your proven cure for heartbreak:

A: _____

B: _____

What do you most remember about your first sexual encounter?

A: _____

B: _____

The weirdest place you have ever woken up:

A: _____

B: _____

What caused your worst hangover?

A: _____ B: _____

Has one of your partners ever thrown a drink in your face?

A: ( ) Yes   ( ) No   B: ( ) Yes   ( ) No

If yes, did you deserve it?

A: ( ) Yes   ( ) No   B: ( ) Yes   ( ) No

If yes or no, what did you say or do to provoke it?

A: _____

B: _____

Something sexual that you would like to try with your partner:

A: _____

B: _____

Are you still in touch with any of your exes?

    A: ( ) Yes ( ) No   B: ( ) Yes ( ) No

If yes, how many of them?

A: _____

B: _____

How do you feel when you hear your partner talking to an ex:

A: ( ) You mind   B: ( ) You mind

     ( ) You don't mind   ( ) You don't mind

     ( ) You pretend that you don't mind   ( ) You pretend that you don't mind

Is there an unrequited love in your life?

    A: ( ) Yes ( ) No   B: ( ) Yes ( ) No

If yes, who?

A: _____

B: _____

Is fantasizing about an ex a form of infidelity?

    A: ( ) Yes ( ) No   B: ( ) Yes ( ) No

You have lied in one of your previous relationships.

    A: ( ) Yes ( ) No   B: ( ) Yes ( ) No

If yes, in how many of them?

A: _____

B: _____

The most expensive gift you ever gave to an ex:

A: Item: _____ Sticker price: _____

B: Item: _____ Sticker price: _____

How many times have you been dumped?

A: ( ) Never   B: ( ) Never

    ( ) 1–5 times   ( ) 1–5 times

    ( ) 10–20 times   ( ) 10–20 times

    ( ) You lost track   ( ) You lost track

How many people have you dumped?

A: ( ) Never   B: ( ) Never

    ( ) 1–5 times   ( ) 1–5 times

    ( ) 10–20 times   ( ) 10–20 times

    ( ) You lost track   ( ) You lost track

Your most satisfying breakup?

A: _____

B: _____

Have you ever been engaged?

    A: ( ) Yes   ( ) No   B: ( ) Yes   ( ) No

If yes, to whom?

A: _____

B: _____

What was the reason for the breakup?

A: _____

B: _____

Have you ever regretted your decision?

    A: ( ) Yes ( ) No   B: ( ) Yes ( ) No

If yes, for what reason?

A: _____

B: _____

If you saw that person walking down the street, what would be the first thought that comes to mind?

A: _____

B: _____

Three things that your friends like about your partner:

A: 1 _____

2 _____

3 _____

B: 1 _____

2 _____

3 _____

Three people you suddenly felt distant from when you fell in love with your partner:

A: 1 _____

2 _____

3 _____

B: 1 _____

2 _____

3 _____

Three things you wish you never knew about your partner's previous life:

A: 1 _____

     2 _____

     3 _____

B: 1 _____

     2 _____

     3 _____

Three qualities you wish your partner had:

A: 1 _____

     2 _____

     3 _____

B: 1 _____

     2 _____

     3 _____

Three things you hope will never happen to your relationship:

A: 1 _____

     2 _____

     3 _____

B: 1 _____

     2 _____

     3 _____

Three of your partner's traits that have attracted you:

A: 1 _____

     2 _____

     3 _____

B: 1 _____

     2 _____

     3 _____

ONE, TWO, THREE

Three things you wish your partner would never say to you again:

A: 1 _____

   2 _____

   3 _____

B: 1 _____

   2 _____

   3 _____

Three things you wish your partner would never do to you again:

A: 1 _____

   2 _____

   3 _____

B: 1 _____

   2 _____

   3 _____

Three things you dislike about being in a relationship:

A: 1 _____

     2 _____

     3 _____

B: 1 _____

     2 _____

     3 _____

Three things you like about being in a relationship:

A: 1 _____

     2 _____

     3 _____

B: 1 _____

     2 _____

     3 _____

TURN-ONS AND TURN-OFFS

The questions of this section are not meant to be considered in a strictly sexual sense.
Rather, respond to them as preferences you might display under the right conditions.

Shopping.

    A: ( ) Turn-on ( ) Turn-off   B: ( ) Turn-on ( ) Turn-off

Mysteries and surprises.

    A: ( ) Turn-on ( ) Turn-off   B: ( ) Turn-on ( ) Turn-off

House of Cards.

    A: ( ) Turn-on ( ) Turn-off   B: ( ) Turn-on ( ) Turn-off

Firemen or nurses.

    A: ( ) Turn-on ( ) Turn-off   B: ( ) Turn-on ( ) Turn-off

VIP.

    A: ( ) Turn-on ( ) Turn-off   B: ( ) Turn-on ( ) Turn-off

Health clubs.

    A: ( ) Turn-on ( ) Turn-off   B: ( ) Turn-on ( ) Turn-off

Cars.

    A: ( ) Turn-on ( ) Turn-off   B: ( ) Turn-on ( ) Turn-off

ABBA.

    A: ( ) Turn-on ( ) Turn-off   B: ( ) Turn-on ( ) Turn-off

Beaches.

    A: ( ) Turn-on ( ) Turn-off   B: ( ) Turn-on ( ) Turn-off

Fur.

    A: ( ) Turn-on ( ) Turn-off   B: ( ) Turn-on ( ) Turn-off

Musicals and plays.

    A: ( ) Turn-on ( ) Turn-off   B: ( ) Turn-on ( ) Turn-off

Power.

    A: ( ) Turn-on ( ) Turn-off   B: ( ) Turn-on ( ) Turn-off

Cigars.

    A: ( ) Turn-on ( ) Turn-off   B: ( ) Turn-on ( ) Turn-off

Talk shows.

    A: ( ) Turn-on ( ) Turn-off   B: ( ) Turn-on ( ) Turn-off

Leather.

    A: ( ) Turn-on   ( ) Turn-off   B: ( ) Turn-on   ( ) Turn-off

Gambling.

    A: ( ) Turn-on   ( ) Turn-off   B: ( ) Turn-on   ( ) Turn-off

Ambition.

    A: ( ) Turn-on   ( ) Turn-off   B: ( ) Turn-on   ( ) Turn-off

Muscles.

    A: ( ) Turn-on   ( ) Turn-off   B: ( ) Turn-on   ( ) Turn-off

Oysters.

    A: ( ) Turn-on   ( ) Turn-off   B: ( ) Turn-on   ( ) Turn-off

Rolling Stones.

    A: ( ) Turn-on   ( ) Turn-off   B: ( ) Turn-on   ( ) Turn-off

Rose gold.

    A: ( ) Turn-on   ( ) Turn-off   B: ( ) Turn-on   ( ) Turn-off

Racing.

    A: ( ) Turn-on   ( ) Turn-off   B: ( ) Turn-on   ( ) Turn-off

Freckles.

    A: ( ) Turn-on   ( ) Turn-off   B: ( ) Turn-on   ( ) Turn-off

Glasses.

    A: ( ) Turn-on   ( ) Turn-off   B: ( ) Turn-on   ( ) Turn-off

Bikers.

    A: ( ) Turn-on   ( ) Turn-off   B: ( ) Turn-on   ( ) Turn-off

Hats.

    A: ( ) Turn-on   ( ) Turn-off   B: ( ) Turn-on   ( ) Turn-off

Europeans.

    A: ( ) Turn-on   ( ) Turn-off   B: ( ) Turn-on   ( ) Turn-off

Sometimes you worry that you are missing out on something by staying in this relationship.

A: ( ) Yes   ( ) No   B: ( ) Yes   ( ) No

If yes, what?

A: _____

B: _____

One thing you like about your body:

A: _____

B: _____

One thing you dislike about your body:

A: _____

B: _____

An emotion you like in yourself:

A: _____

B: _____

An emotion you dislike in yourself:

A: _____

B: _____

Do you sometimes dream about a lost love?

    A: ( ) Yes ( ) No   B: ( ) Yes ( ) No

You committed an indiscretion on a vacation or business trip that you have never revealed to your partner.

    A: ( ) Yes ( ) No   B: ( ) Yes ( ) No

If yes, was it serious?

    A: ( ) Just a flirtation   ( ) Just a kiss
        ( ) Petting, no intercourse   ( ) Unfortunately, very

    B: ( ) Just a flirtation   ( ) Just a kiss
        ( ) Petting, no intercourse   ( ) Unfortunately, very

After it happened, was your partner suspicious?

    A: ( ) Yes ( ) No   B: ( ) Yes ( ) No

If something your partner did or did not do—or said or did not say—upsets you,

A: ( ) you confront your partner immediately.

( ) you wait for the right moment.

( ) you cool down and usually keep it to yourself.

B: ( ) you confront your partner immediately

( ) you wait for the right moment.

( ) you cool down and usually keep it to yourself.

A physical characteristic of your partner's you find attractive:

A: _____   B: _____

A physical characteristic of your partner's you find unattractive:

A: _____   B: _____

Do you agree with your partner's choice of career?

A: ( ) Yes ( ) No   B: ( ) Yes ( ) No

If no, what would you rather have your partner do?

A: _____   B: _____

KIDS

*Even if you do not have children, answer the questions in this section,
since many of them can be considered hypothetically.*

Children like you.

    A: ( ) Yes ( ) No   B: ( ) Yes ( ) No

Do you think your partner is or would make a wonderful mother or father?

    A: ( ) Yes ( ) No   B: ( ) Yes ( ) No

Would you prefer to have a girl or a boy as your first or next child?

    A: ( ) Yes ( ) No   B: ( ) Yes ( ) No

What is the reason for your choice?

A: _____

B: _____

Your favorite names for a girl and a boy:

A: Girl: _____   Boy: _____

B: Girl: _____   Boy: _____

What is the hardest part of being a mother?

A: _____

B: _____

What is the hardest part of being a father?

A: _____

B: _____

If you found your child's diary, would you read it?

    A: ( ) Yes ( ) No   B: ( ) Yes ( ) No

If you do not have kids, can you imagine having kids with your partner?

    A: ( ) Yes ( ) No   B: ( ) Yes ( ) No

If no, why not?

A: _____

B: _____

If yes, who would probably spend more time with them?

    A: ( ) Yes ( ) No   B: ( ) Yes ( ) No

Who will teach your children about sex?

    A: ( ) You ( ) Your partner ( ) Both ( ) Neither
    B: ( ) You ( ) Your partner ( ) Both ( ) Neither

What game or toy from your childhood do you most look forward to playing with a child of your own?

A: _____   B: _____

What lost aspect of your youth do you think a child could restore in you?

A: _____

B: _____

As a teenager, what is the most surprising thing about being in love?

A: _____

B: _____

As an adult, what is the most surprising thing about being in love?

A: _____

B: _____

When you were little, at what age did you think you would get married?

A: _____ B: _____

Something you gave up or put aside when you fell in love with your partner:

A: _____ B: _____

Have you ever stalked or killed a wild animal?

A: ( ) Yes   ( ) No   B: ( ) Yes   ( ) No

If you found out that your partner was having an affair, would you leave the relationship?

A: ( ) Yes   ( ) No   B: ( ) Yes   ( ) No

If not, how would you recover trust?

A: _____

B: _____

What would you give to rid yourself of guilt forever?

A: _____

B: _____

If you could teach your partner one thing with the snap of your fingers, what would it be?

A: _____

B: _____

The longest period of time your partner has been away:

A: _____   B: _____

What did you struggle with most during that time?

A: _____

B: _____

What did you enjoy most during that time?

A: _____

B: _____

How long would you wait for your partner if she or he had to go away?

A: _____   B: _____

Something in your relationship that used to bother you that you have learned to overcome:

A: _____

B: _____

Something about yourself that used to bother you that you have learned to accept:

A: _____

B: _____

A thing or a person you would like to be in your next life:

A: _____   B: _____

YES OR NO

You are moody in the morning.

A: ( ) Yes ( ) No   B: ( ) Yes ( ) No

Too much tolerance can damage a relationship.

A: ( ) Yes ( ) No   B: ( ) Yes ( ) No

Women first.

A: ( ) Yes ( ) No   B: ( ) Yes ( ) No

Baby corn freaks you out.

A: ( ) Yes ( ) No   B: ( ) Yes ( ) No

You feel better about your relationship when you are not in your partner's presence.

A: ( ) Yes ( ) No   B: ( ) Yes ( ) No

Life is fair.

A: ( ) Yes ( ) No   B: ( ) Yes ( ) No

You are rarely bored with your partner.

A: ( ) Yes ( ) No   B: ( ) Yes ( ) No

You are a terrible dancer.

    A: ( ) Yes ( ) No   B: ( ) Yes ( ) No

Men need to be treated like children.

    A: ( ) Yes ( ) No   B: ( ) Yes ( ) No

You have recently stolen something.

    A: ( ) Yes ( ) No   B: ( ) Yes ( ) No

It is possible to be in love with more than one person at the same time.

    A: ( ) Yes ( ) No   B: ( ) Yes ( ) No

Your partner regularly makes you blush.

    A: ( ) Yes ( ) No   B: ( ) Yes ( ) No

You often feel pressured by your partner.

    A: ( ) Yes ( ) No   B: ( ) Yes ( ) No

A couple should live together before marriage.

    A: ( ) Yes ( ) No   B: ( ) Yes ( ) No

You can lie with a straight face.

A: ( ) Yes ( ) No   B: ( ) Yes ( ) No

You enjoy spending time alone with your partner.

A: ( ) Yes ( ) No   B: ( ) Yes ( ) No

You have read de Saint-Exupéry's *The Little Prince.*

A: ( ) Yes ( ) No   B: ( ) Yes ( ) No

You pee in the shower.

A: ( ) Yes ( ) No   B: ( ) Yes ( ) No

You prefer honesty, even when it hurts.

A: ( ) Yes ( ) No   B: ( ) Yes ( ) No

You have participated in a ménage à trois.

A: ( ) Yes ( ) No   B: ( ) Yes ( ) No

You cry when you feel like crying.

A: ( ) Yes ( ) No   B: ( ) Yes ( ) No

Marriage is forever.

    A: ( ) Yes ( ) No   B: ( ) Yes ( ) No

Only perfect people can criticize others.

    A: ( ) Yes ( ) No   B: ( ) Yes ( ) No

You can handle stress.

    A: ( ) Yes ( ) No   B: ( ) Yes ( ) No

Uncapped toothpaste causes problems.

    A: ( ) Yes ( ) No   B: ( ) Yes ( ) No

Love is a battlefield.

    A: ( ) Yes ( ) No   B: ( ) Yes ( ) No

Your partner's body odor gives you a thrill.

    A: ( ) Yes ( ) No   B: ( ) Yes ( ) No

Same-sex marriage is only fair.

    A: ( ) Yes ( ) No   B: ( ) Yes ( ) No

You watch too much TV.

    A: ( ) Yes   ( ) No   B: ( ) Yes   ( ) No

Women enjoy sex as much as men.

    A: ( ) Yes   ( ) No   B: ( ) Yes   ( ) No

You keep work and private time separate.

    A: ( ) Yes   ( ) No   B: ( ) Yes   ( ) No

You still enjoy seducing your partner.

    A: ( ) Yes   ( ) No   B: ( ) Yes   ( ) No

You are often tired.

    A: ( ) Yes   ( ) No   B: ( ) Yes   ( ) No

Sex is the most important part of a relationship.

    A: ( ) Yes   ( ) No   B: ( ) Yes   ( ) No

You sometimes feel sorry for your partner.

    A: ( ) Yes   ( ) No   B: ( ) Yes   ( ) No

You spend too much time in the bathroom.

     A: ( ) Yes   ( ) No   B: ( ) Yes   ( ) No

Other than now, you rarely ask your partner anything.

     A: ( ) Yes   ( ) No   B: ( ) Yes   ( ) No

You help to clean the house.

     A: ( ) Yes   ( ) No   B: ( ) Yes   ( ) No

You smother your partner.

     A: ( ) Yes   ( ) No   B: ( ) Yes   ( ) No

Complaining is a release.

     A: ( ) Yes   ( ) No   B: ( ) Yes   ( ) No

You often wonder why you are in this relationship.

     A: ( ) Yes   ( ) No   B: ( ) Yes   ( ) No

You could be happy with your partner living in a box.

     A: ( ) Yes   ( ) No   B: ( ) Yes   ( ) No

Your partner is too hairy.

     A: ( ) Yes ( ) No   B: ( ) Yes ( ) No

You can learn to be happy without your partner.

     A: ( ) Yes ( ) No   B: ( ) Yes ( ) No

Your partner makes you feel attractive.

     A: ( ) Yes ( ) No   B: ( ) Yes ( ) No

James Bond is sexy.

     A: ( ) Yes ( ) No   B: ( ) Yes ( ) No

At times you have hated your partner.

     A: ( ) Yes ( ) No   B: ( ) Yes ( ) No

You appreciate hearing your partner's opinions.

     A: ( ) Yes ( ) No   B: ( ) Yes ( ) No

You can share in your partner's happiness.

     A: ( ) Yes ( ) No   B: ( ) Yes ( ) No

You feel better when you have a tan.

    A: ( ) Yes ( ) No   B: ( ) Yes ( ) No

Your partner is the more interesting person.

    A: ( ) Yes ( ) No   B: ( ) Yes ( ) No

Something you are now prepared to reveal to your partner:

A: _____

B: _____

Your greatest regret:

A: _____

B: _____

The last time you thought it might be nice to be single again:

A: _____   B: _____

Do you take drugs without your partner's knowledge?

    A: ( ) Yes ( ) No   B: ( ) Yes ( ) No

If yes, what drugs do you take?

A: ( ) Cocaine ( ) Speed ( ) Acid ( ) Marijuana ( ) Painkillers
( ) Ecstasy ( ) Mushrooms ( ) Valium ( ) Heroin

( ) Other: _____

B: ( ) Cocaine ( ) Speed ( ) Acid ( ) Marijuana ( ) Painkillers
( ) Ecstasy ( ) Mushrooms ( ) Valium ( ) Heroin

( ) Other: _____

Do you think that you are addicted to this drug?

A: ( ) Yes ( ) No   B: ( ) Yes ( ) No

The worst present your partner gave you that you pretended to like:

A: _____

B: _____

Did you ever give your partner a gift that you also gave to an ex?

A: ( ) Yes ( ) No   B: ( ) Yes ( ) No

If yes, why didn't you come up with something original?

A: _____

B: _____

Someone who might have been the perfect mate for you, but was already taken:

A: _____   B: _____

You have never told your partner that you were involved with someone else
at the time you met.

     A: ( ) Yes ( ) No   B: ( ) Yes ( ) No

If you met your partner soon after a breakup, did you think of yourself
as being on the rebound?

     A: ( ) Yes ( ) No   B: ( ) Yes ( ) No

Was there ever a point in your current relationship when you thought about breaking up?

     A: ( ) Yes ( ) No   B: ( ) Yes ( ) No

If yes, for what reason?

A: _____

B: _____

If yes, did you tell your partner what you were thinking?

    A: ( ) Yes ( ) No   B: ( ) Yes ( ) No

If yes, what made you continue in the relationship?

A: _____

B: _____

Do you feel better now?

    A: ( ) Yes ( ) No   B: ( ) Yes ( ) No

A talent your partner has of which you are jealous:

A: _____   B: _____

Your pet sometimes means more to you than your partner.

    A: ( ) Yes ( ) No   B: ( ) Yes ( ) No

For this one reason alone you should have left your partner:

    A: ( ) For answering the last question with a yes

          ( ) Other:

    B: ( ) For answering the last question with a yes

          ( ) Other:

For this reason alone you should never leave your partner:

A: _____

B: _____

Assign a percentage value to the truth of the following statements:

You stay in this relationship out of habit.

    A: ( ) 0%   ( ) 25%   ( ) 50%   ( ) 75%   ( ) 100%
    B: ( ) 0%   ( ) 25%   ( ) 50%   ( ) 75%   ( ) 100%

You stay in this relationship because you cannot face dating again.

    A: ( ) 0%   ( ) 25%   ( ) 50%   ( ) 75%   ( ) 100%
    B: ( ) 0%   ( ) 25%   ( ) 50%   ( ) 75%   ( ) 100%

You stay in this relationship because you are afraid of losing your social circle.

A:　( ) 0%　　( ) 25%　　( ) 50%　　( ) 75%　　( ) 100%
B:　( ) 0%　　( ) 25%　　( ) 50%　　( ) 75%　　( ) 100%

You stay in this relationship for the sake of your children.

A:　( ) 0%　　( ) 25%　　( ) 50%　　( ) 75%　　( ) 100%
B:　( ) 0%　　( ) 25%　　( ) 50%　　( ) 75%　　( ) 100%

You fell for your partner for reasons of beauty.

A:　( ) 0%　　( ) 25%　　( ) 50%　　( ) 75%　　( ) 100%
B:　( ) 0%　　( ) 25%　　( ) 50%　　( ) 75%　　( ) 100%

You fell for your partner for economic reasons.

A:　( ) 0%　　( ) 25%　　( ) 50%　　( ) 75%　　( ) 100%
B:　( ) 0%　　( ) 25%　　( ) 50%　　( ) 75%　　( ) 100%

You fell for your partner's sense of humor.

A:　( ) 0%　　( ) 25%　　( ) 50%　　( ) 75%　　( ) 100%
B:　( ) 0%　　( ) 25%　　( ) 50%　　( ) 75%　　( ) 100%

You fell for your partner because you have a father or mother complex.

A: ( ) 0%   ( ) 25%   ( ) 50%   ( ) 75%   ( ) 100%

B: ( ) 0%   ( ) 25%   ( ) 50%   ( ) 75%   ( ) 100%

You fell for your partner out of loneliness.

A: ( ) 0%   ( ) 25%   ( ) 50%   ( ) 75%   ( ) 100%

B: ( ) 0%   ( ) 25%   ( ) 50%   ( ) 75%   ( ) 100%

You fell for your partner because of shared religious beliefs.

A: ( ) 0%   ( ) 25%   ( ) 50%   ( ) 75%   ( ) 100%

B: ( ) 0%   ( ) 25%   ( ) 50%   ( ) 75%   ( ) 100%

You fell for your partner out of curiosity.

A: ( ) 0%   ( ) 25%   ( ) 50%   ( ) 75%   ( ) 100%

B: ( ) 0%   ( ) 25%   ( ) 50%   ( ) 75%   ( ) 100%

You fell for your partner for reasons of social class.

A: ( ) 0%   ( ) 25%   ( ) 50%   ( ) 75%   ( ) 100%

B: ( ) 0%   ( ) 25%   ( ) 50%   ( ) 75%   ( ) 100%

You fell for your partner because of the great sex.

    A: ( ) 0%   ( ) 25%   ( ) 50%   ( ) 75%   ( ) 100%

    B: ( ) 0%   ( ) 25%   ( ) 50%   ( ) 75%   ( ) 100%

You fell for your partner because your partner was so well mannered.

    A: ( ) 0%   ( ) 25%   ( ) 50%   ( ) 75%   ( ) 100%

    B: ( ) 0%   ( ) 25%   ( ) 50%   ( ) 75%   ( ) 100%

You fell for your partner because of the adventure of falling in love.

    A: ( ) 0%   ( ) 25%   ( ) 50%   ( ) 75%   ( ) 100%

    B: ( ) 0%   ( ) 25%   ( ) 50%   ( ) 75%   ( ) 100%

If the above factors applied at the beginning of your relationship, do the same reasons still apply?

    A: ( ) Absolutely   ( ) Somewhat

        ( ) Not at all, but it works anyway

    B: ( ) Absolutely   ( ) Somewhat

        ( ) Not at all, but it works anyway

An affair could refresh your relationship.

    A: ( ) Your partner could probably use something like that.

        ( ) You could use one yourself.   ( ) So they say.

        ( ) Never, what an awful thought.   ( ) Your partner is your secret lover.

    B: ( ) Your partner could probably use something like that.

        ( ) You could use one yourself.   ( ) So they say.

        ( ) Never, what an awful thought.   ( ) Your partner is your secret lover.

You seem to repeat patterns formed in past relationships.

    A: ( ) Yes ( ) No   B: ( ) Yes ( ) No

If yes, what is the most persistent pattern?

A: _____

B: _____

A side of yourself that is revealed when you and your partner are apart:

A: _____

B: _____

How many times a day does your partner cross your mind?

    A: ( ) Too many to count   ( ) Several times
          ( ) Once or twice   ( ) Hardly ever

    B: ( ) Too many to count   ( ) Several times

          ( ) Once or twice   ( ) Hardly ever Something your partner says or does that embarrasses you when you are with other people:

A: _____

B: _____

Do you feel proud to introduce your partner to other people?

    A: ( ) Yes ( ) No   B: ( ) Yes ( ) No

Have you ever known better love?

    A: ( ) Yes ( ) No   B: ( ) Yes ( ) No

Now what?

A: _____

B: _____

TIME OFF

Sometimes you would like to be a child again.

      A: ( ) Yes ( ) No   B: ( ) Yes ( ) No

The worst social event you ever attended with your partner:

A: _____

B: _____

One thing you find irritating about your partner when you attend a social event:

A: _____

B: _____

What would you think if you met yourself at a party?

A: _____

B: _____

What are you most likely to complain about in a hotel?

A: _____

B: _____

One thing that you find incredibly loving about your partner when you are on vacation:

A: _____

B: _____

What do you expect from your partner on your anniversary?

A: _____

B: _____

What would you do if you were a woman for one day?

A/B: _____

What would you do if you were a man for one day?

A/B: _____

If you owned a restaurant, what kind of cuisine would you serve?

A: _____   B: _____

Three words that describe your ideal day in bed:

A: 1 _____

    2 _____

    3 _____

B: 1 _____

    2 _____

    3 _____

If you had a ticket for one month in paradise, where would you go?

A: _____   B: _____

Would you take your partner along to paradise?

    A: ( ) Yes   ( ) No   B: ( ) Yes   ( ) No

Who has a better sense of irony?

    A: ( ) You   ( ) Your partner
    B: ( ) You   ( ) Your partner

Your most treasured possession:

A: _____   B: _____

A word or phrase your partner often uses:

A: _____

B: _____

All women like to hear:

A: _____

B: _____

All men like to hear:

A: _____

B: _____

If you are a woman, what is your most masculine ability?

A/B: _____

If you are a man, what is your most feminine ability?

A/B: _____

A woman's greatest fear:

A: _____   B: _____

A man's greatest fear:

A: _____   B: _____

Something you deliberately did to impress your partner in the early days of your relationship:

A: _____

B: _____

Have you ever attended an ex's wedding?

    A: ( ) Yes ( ) No   B: ( ) Yes ( ) No

If yes, what did you feel when you left the wedding?

A: _____

B: _____

What is the most irritating thing your partner has ever asked you to do before bedtime?

A: _____

B: _____

How long did it take for your feelings to shift from "falling in love" to "true love"?

A: _____

B: _____

In what situation did you realize that your partner had gotten older?

A: _____

B: _____

The most flattering thing your partner ever said to you:

A: _____

B: _____

Do you like your partner's friends?

    A: ( ) Yes ( ) No   B: ( ) Yes ( ) No

What makes a woman interesting?

A: _____

B: _____

What makes a man interesting?

A: _____

B: _____

Whose horoscope do you read first?

    A: ( ) Yours ( ) Your partner's
    B: ( ) Yours ( ) Your partner's

When you see your partner across a crowded room it gives you a thrill.

    A: ( ) Yes ( ) No ( ) You never noticed

    B: ( ) Yes ( ) No ( ) You never noticed

Something you are good at that would surprise your partner:

A: _____

B: _____

Your partner doesn't say good night anymore.

    A: ( ) True ( ) False

    B: ( ) True ( ) False

Love means never having to say you are sorry.

    A: ( ) True ( ) False

    B: ( ) True ( ) False

You appreciate it if your partner says "bless you" when you sneeze?

    A: ( ) Yes ( ) You never thought about it

    B: ( ) Yes ( ) You never thought about it

Did you ever wish your partner had a bigger something?

    A: ( ) Yes ( ) No   B: ( ) Yes ( ) No

A piece of clothing that makes your partner look especially unattractive:

A: _____

B: _____

A piece of clothing that makes your partner look especially attractive:

A: _____

B: _____

A piece of wisdom your partner taught you that you will never forget:

A: _____

B: _____

A book, film, or music of your partner's that you dislike:

A: _____

B: _____

If you are a man, choose three things that you envy about women:

( ) Ponytails ( ) Their intuition ( ) Their ability to give birth ( ) Their bodies

( ) Mental strength ( ) Their playfulness ( ) Their emotional capacity ( ) Lingerie

( ) Their protective instinct ( ) Their social complexity ( ) Their romanticism

( ) That they are not ruled by their penises ( ) Their ease with sentimentality

( ) Their ability to admit weakness ( ) Their seductiveness ( ) Their friendships

( ) Their love of communication ( ) The joy they take in beauty and fashion

( ) Their nesting instinct ( ) Their analytical ability ( ) Their charm when tipsy

( ) Their tolerance of male weakness ( ) Their ability to confront problems

( ) Their capacity for sacrifice ( ) Their passion ( ) Their sex appeal ( ) Their pride

If you are a woman, choose three things you envy about men:

( ) Muscles ( ) Their capacity for bluffing ( ) Their toys

( ) Their ability to hold their liquor ( ) Their sense of direction ( ) Their machismo

( ) Their precision ( ) Their one-track minds ( ) Their eyelashes

( ) Their sense of honor ( ) Body odor ( ) Their capacity to repress their emotions

( ) Their simple pleasures ( ) Wrinkles ( ) Their authoritative voices

( ) Their friendships ( ) That they are ruled by their penises

( ) Their uncomplicated fashions ( ) Their relationship with their mothers

( ) Their ability to act childishly ( ) Their love of women ( ) Their way with money

( ) Chest hair ( ) Their weaknesses ( ) Their handiness with tools

( ) Easy weight loss ( ) Their body language ( ) Their pride

( ) Their belief that anything is possible

A word or phrase your partner often uses that annoys you:

A: _____

B: _____

A word or phrase your partner often uses that pleases you:

A: _____

B: _____

Your sexual vice:

A: _____

B: _____

The longest lust can last:

A: _____

B: _____

When was the last time you enjoyed sex with your partner?

A: _____

B: _____

What are you especially good at when it comes to sex?

A: _____

B: _____

In which part of the sex act is your partner least proficient?

A:　( ) Seduction　( ) Foreplay　( ) The act
　　( ) Endurance　( ) Completion　( ) Afterplay

B:　( ) Seduction　( ) Foreplay　( ) The act
　　( ) Endurance　( ) Completion　( ) Afterplay

In a sexual context, it is better

A:　( ) to give.　( ) to receive.
B:　( ) to give.　( ) to receive.

An unusual place where you and your partner have made love:

A: _____

B: _____

Did you ever take advantage of your partner while your partner was asleep?

A:　( ) Yes　( ) No　　B:　( ) Yes　( ) No

If you have ever been injured while making love, what happened?

A: _____

B: _____

What would you like to experience while blindfolded?

A: _____

B: _____

Describe your partner's sex appeal in one sentence:

A: _____

B: _____

Your most vivid memory about losing your virginity:

A: _____

B: _____

Did you talk about safe sex before you and your partner got intimate?

    A: ( ) Yes ( ) No   B: ( ) Yes ( ) No

If no, why didn't you?

A: _____

B: _____

On what side of the bed do you prefer to sleep?

    A: ( ) Left   ( ) Right   ( ) You don't care

    B: ( ) Left   ( ) Right   ( ) You don't care

When you sleep you prefer the windows to be:

    A: ( ) Open   ( ) Closed

    B: ( ) Open   ( ) Closed

Something about the way your partner sleeps that you find odd or cute:

A: _____

B: _____

Who starred in your last sexual dream?

A: _____

B: _____

How many times a week would you like to have sex with your partner?

A: ( ) Once ( ) 3–5 times ( ) At least 10 times
( ) Recently you haven't really enjoyed sex all that much

B: ( ) Once ( ) 3–5 times ( ) At least 10 times
( ) Recently you haven't really enjoyed sex all that much

Which of the following conditions affects the quality of your sex life?

A: ( ) Tiredness ( ) Time ( ) Stress

( ) Other: _____

B: ( ) Tiredness ( ) Time ( ) Stress

( ) Other: _____

You can have great sex without being drunk or high.

A: ( ) Yes ( ) No B: ( ) Yes ( ) No

Do you sometimes fantasize about having sex with someone else while having sex with your partner?

A: ( ) You would be lying if you said no ( ) No
B: ( ) You would be lying if you said no ( ) No

How does your answer make you feel?

A: _____

B: _____

If your partner wants sex and you don't, are you able to say no?

    A: ( ) Yes ( ) No   B: ( ) Yes ( ) No

How many drinks can you have and still have good sex?

    A: ( ) 1–3 ( ) 3 or more ( ) You're an alcoholic
    B: ( ) 1–3 ( ) 3 or more ( ) You're an alcoholic

The most number of times you have had sex with your partner in a 24-hour period:

A: _____

B: _____

A sexual aid you secretly use that you would now like to bring to your partner's attention:

A: _____

B: _____

Under what conditions did you watch your first X-rated movie (*choose as many as you need*)?

A: ( ) Alone ( ) With a friend ( ) With your partner ( ) In a movie theater
( ) Dressed ( ) Undressed ( ) Excited ( ) Disgusted ( ) Unimpressed

B: ( ) Alone ( ) With a friend ( ) With your partner ( ) In a movie theater
( ) Dressed ( ) Undressed ( ) Excited ( ) Disgusted ( ) Unimpressed

You are sexually uninhibited with your partner.

A: ( ) Yes ( ) No B: ( ) Yes ( ) No

If yes, is there something you haven't yet done?

A: _____

B: _____

If no, name one sexual act that you're unwilling to try under any circumstances:

A: _____

B: _____

Who gets more pleasure out of a quickie?

      A: ( ) You   ( ) Your partner

      B: ( ) You   ( ) Your partner

How does it make you feel when your partner is in a phase of diminished sexual desire?

A: _____

B: _____

At what age do you think you will no longer be interested in sex?

A: _____   B: _____

Someone you find unconventionally sexy:

A: _____

B: _____

Under what conditions is your partner most likely to say "I love you"?

A: _____

B: _____

The most horrifying couple you know:

A: _____

B: _____

A proverb or saying that best describes your relationship:

A: _____

B: _____

If you could have a magical power what would it be?

A: _____

B: _____

One thing you have experienced with your partner that would shock your parents:

A: _____

B: _____

Which of the following five objects remind you most of your partner?

    A: ( ) Umbrella   ( ) Cell phone   ( ) Pencil
            ( ) Light bulb   ( ) Loaf of bread

    B: ( ) Umbrella   ( ) Cell phone   ( ) Pencil
            ( ) Light bulb   ( ) Loaf of bread

Try to describe the reason for your choice in one sentence:

A: _____

B: _____

Which color best describes your sexual relationship?

A: _____

B: _____

What word best matches the color you have picked?

A: _____

B: _____

The oddest thing you have ever put in your mouth:

A: _____

B: _____

The animal your partner most closely resembles:

A: _____   B: _____

Please create a company name for your relationship:

A: _____

B: _____

PLAYTIME

In the space below, spontaneously create a flag that represents your personality.

A:

B:

Try to answer with one word how you deal with your partner's

A: anger: _____   fear: _____

friends: _____   depression: _____

jealousy: _____   family: _____

anxiety: _____   insanity: _____

cruelty: _____   irresponsibility: _____

sadness: _____   moodiness: _____

impatience: _____   distraction: _____

B: anger: _____   fear: _____

friends: _____   depression: _____

jealousy: _____   family: _____

anxiety: _____   insanity: _____

cruelty: _____   irresponsibility: _____

sadness: _____   moodiness: _____

impatience: _____   distraction: _____

ISSUES AND US

An instance of emotional blackmail in your relationship:

A: _____

B: _____

The most dramatic moment in your relationship:

A: _____

B: _____

How do you react when your partner cancels plans?

A: _____

B: _____

What was your greatest concern about introducing your partner to your parents?

A: _____

B: _____

What word or sentence do you most often use to end an argument?

A: _____

B: _____

Define sin:

A: _____

B: _____

Define commitment:

A: _____

B: _____

Do you believe truth is an absolute?

    A: ( ) Yes ( ) No   B: ( ) Yes ( ) No

You know that your friend's partner is cheating, but your friend is not aware of it.

    A: ( ) You tell your friend   ( ) You keep it to yourself
    B: ( ) You tell your friend   ( ) You keep it to yourself

The greatest pain your partner has caused you:

A: _____

B: _____

When you feel the need to assign blame, do you tend to blame yourself?

A: ( ) Yes   ( ) No   B: ( ) Yes   ( ) No

If you had a major problem in your relationship, who would you most likely consult?

A: ( ) A couples counselor   ( ) A psychic or astrologer
( ) A priest or rabbi   ( ) Your mother   ( ) Your father
( ) A psychotherapist   ( ) A friend   ( ) An advice columnist
( ) Your guru   ( ) No one

( ) Other: _____

B: ( ) A couples counselor   ( ) A psychic or astrologer
( ) A priest or rabbi   ( ) Your mother   ( ) Your father
( ) A psychotherapist   ( ) A friend   ( ) An advice columnist
( ) Your guru   ( ) No one

( ) Other: _____

Were you recently jealous but did not let your partner know about it?

A: ( ) Yes   ( ) No   B: ( ) Yes   ( ) No

What was the craziest thing you have done to get your partner's attention in a moment of extreme jealousy?

A: _____

B: _____

The cause of your dumbest argument:

A: _____

B: _____

Who is the more rational one during heated arguments?

A:　( ) Your partner　( ) Yourself　( ) You are equally rational
　　( ) You're equally irrational

B:　( ) Your partner　( ) Yourself　( ) You are equally rational
　　( ) You're equally irrational

Your opinion on separate bathrooms:

A: ( ) A great idea, if you had more space.   ( ) You love to share.

( ) Unfortunately, you have no choice but to share.   ( ) Nonsense.

( ) You already have one of your own.   ( ) You never thought about it.

( ) Some of your best fights start in the bathroom.

B: ( ) A great idea, if you had more space.   ( ) You love to share.

( ) Unfortunately, you have no choice but to share.   ( ) Nonsense.

( ) You already have one of your own.   ( ) You never thought about it.

( ) Some of your best fights start in the bathroom.

Do you take any form of abuse from your partner?

A: ( ) Yes   ( ) No   B: ( ) Yes   ( ) No

If yes, what kind of abuse?

A: ( ) Physical   ( ) Verbal   ( ) Emotional

B: ( ) Physical   ( ) Verbal   ( ) Emotional

How often do you think you suffer abuse?

A: ( ) Once a week   ( ) More than once a week   ( ) Once a month
( ) More than once a month   ( ) Once a year   ( ) A few times a year
( ) Only once   ( ) Never   ( ) You would never stay in an abusive relationship

B: ( ) Once a week   ( ) More than once a week   ( ) Once a month
( ) More than once a month   ( ) Once a year   ( ) A few times a year
( ) Only once   ( ) Never   ( ) You would never stay in an abusive relationship

You expect more from your partner.

A: ( ) Yes   ( ) No   B: ( ) Yes   ( ) No

If yes, what is it that you expect?

A: _____

B: _____

When you hear your partner humming, whistling, or singing,

A: ( ) it makes you happy.   ( ) it drives you crazy.
B: ( ) it makes you happy.   ( ) it drives you crazy.

Choose three of the following recommendations for your partner:

A: ( ) Shower every day   ( ) Be more patient

( ) Relax and breathe   ( ) Compromise more

( ) Enjoy life   ( ) Spend more time with yourself

( ) Don't do drugs   ( ) Be more open-minded

( ) Be more responsible   ( ) Don't always have the last word

( ) Solve that dandruff problem   ( ) See a doctor or dentist

( ) Drink less   ( ) See the good in people   ( ) See a therapist

( ) Have a little less attitude   ( ) Be true to yourself

B: ( ) Shower every day   ( ) Be more patient

( ) Relax and breathe   ( ) Compromise more

( ) Enjoy life   ( ) Spend more time with yourself

( ) Don't do drugs   ( ) Be more open-minded

( ) Be more responsible   ( ) Don't always have the last word

( ) Solve that dandruff problem   ( ) See a doctor or dentist

( ) Drink less   ( ) See the good in people   ( ) See a therapist

( ) Have a little less attitude   ( ) Be true to yourself

What item of your partner's would you hope to sell first in a garage sale?

A: _____

B: _____

The rudest thing you ever said to your partner:

A: _____

B: _____

Do you believe the silent treatment is an effective method of expressing displeasure?

    A: ( ) Yes ( ) No   B: ( ) Yes ( ) No

Who gives more to the relationship?

    A: ( ) You ( ) Your partner ( ) You both give equally
    B: ( ) You ( ) Your partner ( ) You both give equally

Who is more willing to settle an argument?

    A: ( ) You ( ) Your partner
    B: ( ) You ( ) Your partner

A recurring dream:

A: _____

B: _____

Did you ever behave like a stalker when you were obsessed with someone?

    A: ( ) Yes ( ) No   B: ( ) Yes ( ) No

Which bad habit from your childhood do you still have?

A: _____

B: _____

In your current relationship, you behave more like

    A: ( ) your mother. ( ) your father.

    B: ( ) your mother. ( ) your father.

Which of your mother's bad traits have you uncontrollably adopted?

A: _____

B: _____

Which of your father's bad traits have you uncontrollably adopted?

A: _____

B: _____

To which parent do you feel closer?

    A: ( ) Your mother ( ) Your father ( ) Equally close to both ( ) Neither

    B: ( ) Your mother ( ) Your father ( ) Equally close to both ( ) Neither

How often do you speak to your parents?

A: _____

B: _____

When you were at your most furious, what would you have liked to do to your partner if you could have gotten away with it?

A: _____

B: _____

Your greatest fear about your relationship:

A: _____

B: _____

Are you always able to express the love you feel?

    A: ( ) Yes ( ) No ( ) Only when I feel good about myself

    B: ( ) Yes ( ) No ( ) Only when I feel good about myself

Are your parents still married?

    A: ( ) Yes ( ) No   B: ( ) Yes ( ) No

Did your parents set a bad example with their marriage?

    A: ( ) Yes ( ) No   B: ( ) Yes ( ) No

What scared you about your parents' marriage when you were a child?

A: _____

B: _____

What scared you about your parents' marriage after you left home?

A: _____

B: _____

What did you like about your parents' marriage during the time you lived with them?

A: _____

B: _____

What did you like about your parents' marriage after you left home?

A: _____

B: _____

You believe that your partner needs more love than you can give.

    A: ( ) Yes ( ) No   B: ( ) Yes ( ) No

At what times do you find you are most needy?

A: _____

B: _____

At such times, does your partner respond to your neediness?

    A: ( ) Yes ( ) No   B: ( ) Yes ( ) No

Have you ever wished to die?

    A: ( ) Yes ( ) No   B: ( ) Yes ( ) No

You often act like a baby in your relationship.

    A: ( ) Yes ( ) No   B: ( ) Yes ( ) No

If yes, what do you think you will accomplish?

A: _____

B: _____

You sometimes wish you were *(choose two)*

A: ( ) more beautiful.   ( ) stronger.   ( ) famous.   ( ) fearless.
( ) smarter.   ( ) more talented.   ( ) married with children.
( ) rich.   ( ) sophisticated.   ( ) less beautiful.   ( ) less strong.
( ) not famous.   ( ) more careful.   ( ) not as smart.   ( ) less talented.
( ) single with a cell phone.   ( ) less rich.   ( ) more easygoing.

A: ( ) more beautiful.   ( ) stronger.   ( ) famous.   ( ) fearless.
( ) smarter.   ( ) more talented.   ( ) married with children.
( ) rich.   ( ) sophisticated.   ( ) less beautiful.   ( ) less strong.
( ) not famous.   ( ) more careful.   ( ) not as smart.   ( ) less talented.
( ) single with a cell phone.   ( ) less rich.   ( ) more easygoing.

Masturbation is important.

A: ( ) You agree   ( ) You disagree   ( ) You don't know
B: ( ) You agree   ( ) You disagree   ( ) You don't know

Something predictable your partner says or does when you are going to see a movie:

A: _____

B: _____

NEUROSES

Something predictable your partner says or does when you are at the airport:

A: _____

B: _____

Something predictable your partner says or does when you are expecting guests:

A: _____

B: _____

Something predictable your partner says or does when you are about to leave the house:

A: _____

B: _____

Does your partner sometimes seem more like your sister or your brother?

A:　( ) Yes　( ) No　　　B:　( ) Yes　( ) No

CHOICES

Even if you like both or none of the choices, choose one spontaneously.

A:	B:			A:	B:	
( )	( )	Spending	or	( )	( )	saving.
( )	( )	Wine	or	( )	( )	champagne.
( )	( )	Scented candle	or	( )	( )	room spray.
( )	( )	Egypt	or	( )	( )	New Zealand.
( )	( )	Karate	or	( )	( )	piano lessons.
( )	( )	Your partner's parents	or	( )	( )	your parents.
( )	( )	Risk	or	( )	( )	stability.
( )	( )	Smart phone	or	( )	( )	remote control.
( )	( )	Sunbathing	or	( )	( )	hiking.
( )	( )	Holidays with	or	( )	( )	without family.
( )	( )	Dinner	or	( )	( )	party.
( )	( )	Separate residences	or	( )	( )	living together.
( )	( )	Sony	or	( )	( )	Panasonic.
( )	( )	Movie star	or	( )	( )	rock star.
( )	( )	Garden	or	( )	( )	view.
( )	( )	Ravel's "Bolero"	or	( )	( )	The Beatles' "Let It Be."
( )	( )	Gifts	or	( )	( )	attention.
( )	( )	Fireworks	or	( )	( )	thunderstorm.
( )	( )	Om	or	( )	( )	Amen.
( )	( )	Penthouse	or	( )	( )	farmhouse.
( )	( )	Now	or	( )	( )	later.
( )	( )	Breakfast	or	( )	( )	cuddling longer.
( )	( )	Drinking	or	( )	( )	dancing.

CHOICES

A: B:		A: B:	
( ) ( ) Step by step	or	( ) ( ) jump.
( ) ( ) Piercing	or	( ) ( ) tattoo.
( ) ( ) *National Enquirer*	or	( ) ( ) *The New Yorker.*
( ) ( ) Curtains	or	( ) ( ) blinds.
( ) ( ) First Lady and President	or	( ) ( ) Laurel and Hardy.
( ) ( ) Guacamole	or	( ) ( ) hummus.
( ) ( ) Cigarette	or	( ) ( ) bubble gum.
( ) ( ) Ears	or	( ) ( ) toes.
( ) ( ) The seventies	or	( ) ( ) the millennium.
( ) ( ) High five	or	( ) ( ) hug.
( ) ( ) Night owl	or	( ) ( ) early bird.
( ) ( ) Shaved	or	( ) ( ) natural.
( ) ( ) In public places	or	( ) ( ) only at home.
( ) ( ) Bach	or	( ) ( ) Mozart.
( ) ( ) Telling all	or	( ) ( ) keeping secrets.
( ) ( ) Jeans	or	( ) ( ) chinos.
( ) ( ) Scrabble	or	( ) ( ) Monopoly.
( ) ( ) Tantric	or	( ) ( ) Vegas-style.
( ) ( ) *Saturday Night Fever*	or	( ) ( ) *Saturday Night Live.*
( ) ( ) Lighter	or	( ) ( ) matches.
( ) ( ) Something	or	( ) ( ) everything or nothing.
( ) ( ) Appetizer	or	( ) ( ) dessert.
( ) ( ) Halloween	or	( ) ( ) Thanksgiving.

CHOICES

A: B:

( ) ( ) Rain or

( ) ( ) Knight or

( ) ( ) Green tea or

( ) ( ) Taxi or

( ) ( ) Kermit or

( ) ( ) Yoga or

( ) ( ) Roller coaster or

( ) ( ) Guest or

( ) ( ) Johnny Cash or

( ) ( ) Dentist or

( ) ( ) It's all about me or

( ) ( ) Pond or

( ) ( ) Plan or

( ) ( ) Guillotine or

( ) ( ) French fries or

( ) ( ) Paper or

( ) ( ) A good watch or

( ) ( ) Mellow or

( ) ( ) Give in or

( ) ( ) Rubber duck or

( ) ( ) Take it or

A: B:

( ) ( ) crickets.

( ) ( ) angel.

( ) ( ) root beer.

( ) ( ) subway.

( ) ( ) Miss Piggy.

( ) ( ) gardening.

( ) ( ) Ferris wheel.

( ) ( ) host.

( ) ( ) Barbra Streisand.

( ) ( ) in-laws.

( ) ( ) it's all about us.

( ) ( ) waterfall.

( ) ( ) improvisation.

( ) ( ) gallows.

( ) ( ) spaghetti.

( ) ( ) computer screen.

( ) ( ) a good time.

( ) ( ) outgoing.

( ) ( ) give blood.

( ) ( ) sponge.

( ) ( ) leave it.

Your philosophy:

A: _____

B: _____

You are ruled by:

A: _____

B: _____

Your greatest extravagance:

A: _____

B: _____

The best advice someone ever gave you about relationships:

A: _____

B: _____

Have you ever feared for your partner's life?

    A: ( ) Yes ( ) No   B: ( ) Yes ( ) No

Could you imagine caring for your partner after an accident or a severe illness?

    A: ( ) Yes   ( ) No   ( ) You've never thought about it

    B: ( ) Yes   ( ) No   ( ) You've never thought about it

Are you comfortable seeing your partner walk around the house naked?

    A: ( ) Yes   ( ) No   B: ( ) Yes   ( ) No

If no, why not?

A: _____

B: _____

Are you comfortable walking around the house naked while your partner watches you?

    A: ( ) Yes   ( ) No   B: ( ) Yes   ( ) No

If no, why not?

A: _____

B: _____

If you had a remote control to increase, decrease, or mute your partner's character traits, which button would you press?

A:

Generosity:	( ) + ( ) − ( ) Mute	Humor:	( ) + ( ) − ( ) Mute
Knowledge:	( ) + ( ) − ( ) Mute	Compassion:	( ) + ( ) − ( ) Mute
Politeness:	( ) + ( ) − ( ) Mute	Discipline:	( ) + ( ) − ( ) Mute
Imagination:	( ) + ( ) − ( ) Mute	Honesty:	( ) + ( ) − ( ) Mute
Strength:	( ) + ( ) − ( ) Mute	Warmth:	( ) + ( ) − ( ) Mute
Sensuality:	( ) + ( ) − ( ) Mute	Sexuality:	( ) + ( ) − ( ) Mute
Energy:	( ) + ( ) − ( ) Mute	Curiosity:	( ) + ( ) − ( ) Mute
Spontaneity:	( ) + ( ) − ( ) Mute	Faith:	( ) + ( ) − ( ) Mute
Trust:	( ) + ( ) − ( ) Mute	Ambition:	( ) + ( ) − ( ) Mute
Creativity:	( ) + ( ) − ( ) Mute	Thoughtfulness:	( ) + ( ) − ( ) Mute
Playfulness:	( ) + ( ) − ( ) Mute	Moderation:	( ) + ( ) − ( ) Mute
Physical Fitness:	( ) + ( ) − ( ) Mute	Stylishness:	( ) + ( ) − ( ) Mute
Discretion:	( ) + ( ) − ( ) Mute	Sensitivity:	( ) + ( ) − ( ) Mute
Industriousness:	( ) + ( ) − ( ) Mute	Consistency:	( ) + ( ) − ( ) Mute
Loyalty:	( ) + ( ) − ( ) Mute	Sociability:	( ) + ( ) − ( ) Mute
Tolerance:	( ) + ( ) − ( ) Mute	Intellectuality:	( ) + ( ) − ( ) Mute
Toughness:	( ) + ( ) − ( ) Mute	Pride:	( ) + ( ) − ( ) Mute
Humility:	( ) + ( ) − ( ) Mute	Intuition:	( ) + ( ) − ( ) Mute

B:

Generosity:	( ) + ( ) – ( ) Mute	Humor:	( ) + ( ) – ( ) Mute
Knowledge:	( ) + ( ) – ( ) Mute	Compassion:	( ) + ( ) – ( ) Mute
Politeness:	( ) + ( ) – ( ) Mute	Discipline:	( ) + ( ) – ( ) Mute
Imagination:	( ) + ( ) – ( ) Mute	Honesty:	( ) + ( ) – ( ) Mute
Strength:	( ) + ( ) – ( ) Mute	Warmth:	( ) + ( ) – ( ) Mute
Sensuality:	( ) + ( ) – ( ) Mute	Sexuality:	( ) + ( ) – ( ) Mute
Energy:	( ) + ( ) – ( ) Mute	Curiosity:	( ) + ( ) – ( ) Mute
Spontaneity:	( ) + ( ) – ( ) Mute	Faith:	( ) + ( ) – ( ) Mute
Trust:	( ) + ( ) – ( ) Mute	Ambition:	( ) + ( ) – ( ) Mute
Creativity:	( ) + ( ) – ( ) Mute	Thoughtfulness:	( ) + ( ) – ( ) Mute
Playfulness:	( ) + ( ) – ( ) Mute	Moderation:	( ) + ( ) – ( ) Mute
Physical Fitness:	( ) + ( ) – ( ) Mute	Stylishness:	( ) + ( ) – ( ) Mute
Discretion:	( ) + ( ) – ( ) Mute	Sensitivity:	( ) + ( ) – ( ) Mute
Industriousness:	( ) + ( ) – ( ) Mute	Consistency:	( ) + ( ) – ( ) Mute
Loyalty:	( ) + ( ) – ( ) Mute	Sociability:	( ) + ( ) – ( ) Mute
Tolerance:	( ) + ( ) – ( ) Mute	Intellectuality:	( ) + ( ) – ( ) Mute
Toughness:	( ) + ( ) – ( ) Mute	Pride:	( ) + ( ) – ( ) Mute
Humility:	( ) + ( ) – ( ) Mute	Intuition:	( ) + ( ) – ( ) Mute

What would you fear most if you learned that your partner had just won the lottery?

A: _____

B: _____

How would you feel if you suddenly learned that your partner had undergone a change of sexual orientation?

A: _____

B: _____

What do you consider your partner's greatest achievement?

A: _____

B: _____

Your greatest fear:

A: _____

B: _____

You are notorious for:

A: _____

B: _____

Name your poison:

A: _____

B: _____

An embarrassing prejudiced thought:

A: _____

B: _____

A shameful moment in your current relationship:

A: _____

B: _____

A friend's relationship that you envy:

A: _____

B: _____

What was the biggest gamble of your life?

A: _____

B: _____

A flirtation at work that troubles you:

A: _____

B: _____

Your greatest weakness as a friend:

A: _____

B: _____

Who goes out more?

    A: ( ) You   ( ) Your partner   ( ) Other people

    B: ( ) You   ( ) Your partner   ( ) Other people

An aggressive move you made in your current relationship:

A: _____

B: _____

The greatest risk you have taken in your current relationship:

A: _____

B: _____

Have you consulted a psychic because of your current relationship?

    A: ( ) Yes ( ) No   B: ( ) Yes ( ) No

If yes, did you learn something surprising?

A: _____

B: _____

If you could change one of your partner's body parts, what would it be?

A: _____

B: _____

You believe that you are emotionally stronger than your partner.

    A: ( ) Yes ( ) No   B: ( ) Yes ( ) No

If no, does it matter?

    A: ( ) You ( ) Your partner ( ) It might at some point
    B: ( ) You ( ) Your partner ( ) It might at some point

You sometimes stare in the mirror and think your partner is lucky to have you.

    A: ( ) Yes ( ) No   B: ( ) Yes ( ) No

If no, why not?

A: _____

B: _____

Do you take your partner to a restaurant or hotel that you have visited with an ex?

    A: ( ) Yes ( ) No   B: ( ) Yes ( ) No

You sometimes enjoy being mean to your partner.

    A: ( ) Yes ( ) No   B: ( ) Yes ( ) No

If yes, describe a situation that would provoke you to cruelty:

A: _____

B: _____

How many times have you been asked out by another man or woman during your current relationship?

    A: ( ) 0–10 times ( ) 10–25 times ( ) 25–50 times
          ( ) Over 50 times ( ) Only once ( ) Never

    B: ( ) 0–10 times ( ) 10–25 times ( ) 25–50 times
          ( ) Over 50 times ( ) Only once ( ) Never

If "only once" or "never," how did your answer make you feel?

A: _____

B: _____

You provided an alibi for a friend who was having an affair and didn't tell your partner.

    A: ( ) Yes ( ) No   B: ( ) Yes ( ) No

If yes, why didn't you tell your partner about it?

A: _____

B: _____

You have a problem crying in front of your partner.

    A: ( ) Yes ( ) No   B: ( ) Yes ( ) No

When you find someone attractive you instinctively start fantasizing.

    A: ( ) Yes ( ) No   B: ( ) Yes ( ) No

Which of the two of you is higher maintenance?

    A: ( ) You can't afford to be high maintenance.

          ( ) You are higher maintenance.

    B: ( ) You can't afford to be high maintenance.

          ( ) You are higher maintenance.

You have slept with more men or women than you have told your partner.

    A: ( ) Yes   ( ) No   B: ( ) Yes   ( ) No

If yes, how many lovers do you consider too many?

A: _____   B: _____

Would you rather assume the role of sexual student or teacher?

    A: ( ) Student   ( ) Teacher

    B: ( ) Student   ( ) Teacher

When you are away from home you sometimes wish you didn't have to call your partner or family.

    A: ( ) Yes   ( ) No   B: ( ) Yes   ( ) No

You have masturbated at work.

    A: ( ) Yes ( ) No   B: ( ) Yes ( ) No

If yes, why at work?

A: _____

B: _____

THE LONG RUN

*If for whatever reason marriage is not an option, substitute
"long-term commitment" for "marriage" where appropriate.*

What is your mission in life?

A: _____

B: _____

What is the most important thing to consider when contemplating marriage?

A: _____

B: _____

If you are married, do you feel more mature since you got married?

      A: ( ) Yes   ( ) No   B: ( ) Yes   ( ) No

If yes, why?

A: _____

B: _____

If you had to make an instant decision, whom of all the people you know (besides your partner) would you choose to spend the rest of your life with?

A: _____

B: _____

One of your partner's friends that should not attend your wedding:

A: _____

B: _____

Describe how you see your partner ten years from now:

A: _____

B: _____

If you are married, did you ever consider calling off the wedding?

A: ( ) Yes ( ) No   B: ( ) Yes ( ) No

What would you do if you were unable to work for a long period of time?

A: _____

B: _____

Something you see in the future of your relationship that causes you concern:

A: _____

B: _____

Something you see in the future of your relationship that brings you joy:

A: _____

B: _____

Something you see in your partner's future that causes you concern:

A: _____

B: _____

Something you see in your partner's future that makes you happy:

A: _____

B: _____

A habit of your partner's that you have proudly accepted:

A: _____

B: _____

A habit of your partner's that you must learn to accept:

A: _____

B: _____

If you are not married, the one thing you need to hear from your partner before you are willing to tie the knot:

A: _____

B: _____

Would you sign a prenuptial agreement?

     A: ( ) Yes   ( ) No   B: ( ) Yes   ( ) No

Why or why not?

A: _____

B: _____

Do you think anything is compromised when you accept money from your partner?

     A: ( ) Yes   ( ) No   B: ( ) Yes   ( ) No

If yes, what is compromised?

A: _____

B: _____

Under what conditions do you feel it is acceptable to take money from your partner?

A: _____

B: _____

If you were to die, which of your friends would you like to see your partner remarry?

A: _____

B: _____

What do you hope your partner will have accomplished professionally five years from now?

A: _____

B: _____

What do you hope your partner will have accomplished emotionally five years from now?

A: _____

B: _____

If you have not yet retired, where would you like to retire?

A: _____

B: _____

How do you picture hell?

A: _____

B: _____

How do you picture heaven?

A: _____

B: _____

When you met, it was

    A: ( ) destiny.   ( ) coincidence.   ( ) a good idea.
        ( ) a disaster.   ( ) the result of a conspiracy among your friends.

    B: ( ) destiny.   ( ) coincidence.   ( ) a good idea.
        ( ) a disaster.   ( ) the result of a conspiracy among your friends.

What fortune would you wish your partner to find in a fortune cookie?

A: _____

B: _____

The best reason to stay together:

A: _____

B: _____

The worst reason to stay together:

A: _____

B: _____

If money and time were not an issue, what would be the ideal place to recover after a breakup?

A: _____

B: _____

Considering everything you have learned from this book, you are now convinced

    A: ( ) your partner is still the person of your dreams.

           ( ) your partner should no longer be your partner.

           ( ) you should have never met your partner.

           ( ) you and your partner need counseling.

           ( ) you need to be more independent.

           ( ) sometimes it's better not to know.

           ( ) your relationship is more solid than ever.

    B: ( ) your partner is still the person of your dreams.

           ( ) your partner should no longer be your partner.

           ( ) you should have never met your partner.

           ( ) you and your partner need counseling.

           ( ) you need to be more independent.

           ( ) sometimes it's better not to know.

           ( ) your relationship is more solid than ever.

The best decision you have ever made:

A: _____

B: _____

Your next goal in life:

A: _____

B: _____

NOTES

NOTES

NOTES

NOTES

NOTES

_____

_____

_____

_____

_____

_____

_____

_____

_____

_____

_____

_____

NOTES

NOTES